The Music Scene

The Music Industry

Matt Anniss

FRANKLIN WATTS
LONDON•SYDNEY

This edition published in 2015 by
Franklin Watts
338 Euston Road
London NW1 3BH

Franklin Watts Australia
Level 17/207 Kent Street
Sydney, NSW 2000

Produced by Calcium, www.calciumcreative.co.uk

A CIP catalogue record for this book is available from
the British Library.

ISBN 978 1 4451 3937 1

Dewey classification: 338.4'778164

Printed in China

Franklin Watts is a division of Hachette Children's Books,
an Hachette UK company
www.hachette.co.uk

Acknowledgements:
The publisher would like to thank the following for permission to
reproduce photographs: Alamy: Trinity Mirror / Mirrorpix 32;
Dreamstime: Criber 10, Edgaralanf 37, Featureflash 26b, Flynt 26t,
Furesz 5, 22, Imagecollect 17, Kriscole 34, Monkeybusinessimages 42,
Sbukley 25, Winterling 11t; Rex Features: Mike Hollist / Daily Mail 15,
NBCU Photobank 12, Brian Rasic 19, Skyline Features 40; Shutterstock:
Yuralaits Albert 14, Yuri Arcurs 30l, Blend Images 20, Cinemafestival
31, Andrei Contiu 38, DFree 39, Dpaint 6, Entertainment Press 8, Helga
Esteb 21, Featureflash 43c, Harmony Gerber 33, Péter Gudella 16, Aija
Lehtonen 27, 28, Nejron Photo cover, Iurii Osadchi 9, Losevsky Pavel
30-31, Joe Seer 7, Tristan Scholze 36-37, Stocklight 24, Tsian 11r, Debby
Wong 35; Soundcloud: 43tr.

Every attempt has been made to clear copyright. Should there be any
inadvertent omission please apply to the publisher for rectification.

CONTENTS

ORIGINS OF THE MODERN MUSIC INDUSTRY

The music industry is a vast global machine. It offers opportunities for those with musical, marketing or technical talents to follow their dreams. For every star singer, rapper, DJ or famous band, there are hundreds of people working behind the scenes to make their dreams come true.

Money from music

The music industry is a term used to describe the many different companies and individuals who, in some way, make a living from music. That includes performers, music producers, concert promoters, record labels and music distributors (the people who get music to shops and download stores). Also involved are instrument manufacturers, sound technicians and marketing companies who work hard to promote musicians and music releases.

Humble origins

People have written and played music for thousands of years. Skilled musicians entertained people at all levels of society and earned their living by doing so. All music was live music back then. What we call the music industry really began with the development of equipment that could record sound. The first device was a phonograph, invented by Thomas Edison, in 1877. The machine used strange-looking wax cylinders to record and replay music.

Today's DJs wouldn't exist without the development of equipment for recording and replaying music in the 1870s.

Disc doctor

The development of records (pressed-plastic – or vinyl – discs) allowed people to listen to recorded music at home on a device called a gramophone. Records quickly became popular among wealthy people in the early part of the twentieth century. This created work for musicians, singers and popular entertainers of the time. They recorded their performances onto records so that they could be sold to the public by record labels.

Boom time

Records really began to take off in the 1950s when the equipment to listen to them – known as 'record players' – became cheaper. Teenagers quickly became more interested in pop music and record sales soared.

In the twenty-first century, top singers such as Beyoncé can earn millions of dollars every year.

Global industry

Today, the worldwide music industry is huge. According to the international music industry body (the IFPI), global music sales topped US$15 billion in 2013. That's an enormous amount of money – and it doesn't include sales of concert tickets or 'royalties' (small payments given to songwriters and performers when their songs are played on radio or television). Music is big business, and if you are very successful in the music industry you can become very rich indeed.

Inside story

This book will give you a glimpse into the inner workings of the music industry, explaining who does what and why. We'll also show you how bands go from bedroom enthusiasts to global stars and how television and the Internet changed the music industry forever.

BASEMENT BEGINNINGS

While it may be big business, the majority of people who work in the music industry do not earn a lot of money. For every star earning millions in music sales and concert tours, there are many hundreds of thousands of others who get by on passion and enthusiasm alone.

The journey begins

Most bands, singers and rappers started out in the same way – with a love of music, a bit of talent and a burning ambition to make a career out of it. No one is successful overnight, and behind every big star is a story of humble beginnings. Many have sung for nothing at a local club or formed a band with their friends.

Fifty years on the road

Success doesn't always come quickly. Famous American blues musician Seasick Steve (above) spent 50 years as a musician before he got his big break. Steve was born in 1941 but didn't record his breakthrough debut solo album until 2006, when he was 65 years old! For much of his life, he has travelled around the USA doing casual jobs on farms and playing occasional solo gigs to earn a living. It wasn't until he moved to Europe in 2001 that he was finally 'spotted' and offered a recording contract.

Local legends

There are music scenes in almost every major town and city around the world. These scenes are the lifeblood of the music industry – without them there would be no music industry at all. These local circuits of concert venues, clubs, recording studios and rehearsal rooms are the breeding ground for many future stars. These scenes exist to entertain music fans but also to help fine-tune the skills of aspiring music stars.

Hard slog

Very few musicians ever make a decent living out of their passion. For some, their dreams will be just that – dreams. But for others, success in their town or city is just the beginning of a journey to the very top. Lady Gaga was in an unsuccessful band in New York City for two years before she was signed to a record label. U2 got their break following several years of hard work in their home city of Dublin.

The goss

Some small music venues become world famous for giving bands their big break. Following the success of The Beatles in the 1960s, Liverpool's Cavern Club became a go-to destination for record label talent scouts from London. These scouts thought they would find other local bands that they could turn into stars. Several bands were signed in this way, but none were as successful as The Beatles.

Before they make it big, bands must first build up a loyal local following of fans in their town or city or on the internet.

SPOTTED

The music industry needs a steady flow of fresh talent to create potential stars. Because of this, record label executives, concert promoters and talent scouts are always on the lookout for new artists and sounds. Often, it is the local music scenes to which they look for inspiration.

All about the buzz

If a band becomes popular in their local music scene, it is likely that they'll be asked to play gigs around the country. When this happens, they may begin to attract the attention of record labels. A buzz about a new artist may then develop – whether on the Internet, in underground music circles, or both. When this happens, a record label may send a talent scout to watch the band at a gig in their home town.

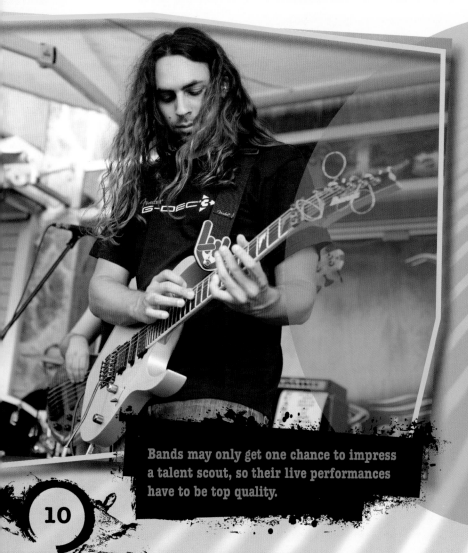

Bands may only get one chance to impress a talent scout, so their live performances have to be top quality.

Scouting for bands

Talent scouts are traditionally employed by record labels and music management companies. They are looking for bands that have that rare combination of an exciting sound, attitude and the right look.

Talent scouts have a wide knowledge of music and are experts in spotting would-be stars. Many bands dream of being watched by a talent scout, because it means they could earn a recording contract worth hundreds of thousands of pounds.

Paranoid Travellers Feb 2012

Sending demo CDs to radio DJs is a great way for young artists to get their music heard by a wider audience.

Demo derby

Some artists are signed to record labels after sending in a demo. This is a homemade CD of songs designed to showcase their talents. It is sometimes given away for free at gigs. Now, many aspiring artists also post their demos on websites such as Facebook, MySpace and SoundCloud in a bid to get 'spotted'.

The goss

Indie-rock stars Arctic Monkeys famously hit the big time on the back of online success. Record labels noticed how many times their songs had been downloaded for free on the MySpace website.

Do it yourself

There are other ways to get noticed and earn a recording contract. In dance music, for example, many artists 'self release' their music. This means they sell it themselves. They usually release tracks on vinyl records or as downloads through specialist online stores such as Bandcamp. If their music sells well and makes an impact, established record labels may offer them a contract.

Radio stars

Many radio stations support new talent by giving up-and-coming artists vital airplay to attract the attention of labels. In the UK, the BBC is very good at doing this, through their local *BBC Introducing* programmes and Radio One's popular *One To Watch* feature. The USA has no equivalent of the BBC, but many local radio stations try to play tracks by up-and-coming bands from their area.

11

The Killers

American band The Killers are now one of the biggest rock bands in the world. Like many artists, they initially struggled to attract interest in their home country. In fact, it took a record label from the other side of the world to give them their big break and put them on the path to superstardom.

The Killers (l to r) Dave Keuning, Brandon Flowers, Ronnie Vannucci and Mark Stoermer.

Las Vegas roots

Brandon Flowers formed The Killers in Las Vegas, USA, in 2001. He had previously been in a number of unsuccessful synth-pop bands. He was inspired to create a new rock group after seeing British band Oasis in concert. The newly-formed band set about building up a loyal following in their home city. They spent two years writing music and playing small venues in an attempt to fine-tune their sound.

Enter the agent

Although their success in these first two years was limited, The Killers learned a lot from their time in Las Vegas. Brandon Flowers was able to turn himself into an inspiring front man and lead singer. All the hard work paid off, because in early 2003 the band caught the eye of visiting talent scout Braden Merrick. He loved the look and sound of the band so much that he offered to be their manager and arranged for them to record a demo.

A buzz builds

The Killers first played gigs in London in August 2003. They quickly became one of the most talked-about bands on the circuit. They were given a boost when BBC Radio One DJ Zane Lowe played their limited edition debut single Mr. Brightside on his show. On the back of this endorsement and their rising popularity, the limited edition single sold out within a week. News of their rapid success in the UK quickly spread to the USA, and The Killers signed to a huge label, Island Def Jam, in early 2004.

Interest from London

The demo was sent to major record labels in the USA. The only record label that took any interest was Warner Brothers, who invited them to play a showcase set. At that set was a representative of Warner Brothers UK, who passed the band's demo on to a small independent label in London called Lizard King. Label boss Martin Heath loved what he heard, and signed up The Killers in July 2003.

TIMELINE: The Killers

2001: Brandon Flowers goes to an Oasis gig and is inspired to form a band

2003: Release the limited edition debut single *Mr. Brightside*

2004: The Killers sign to Island Def Jam in the USA

2008: They headline the Reading and Leeds festivals

2010: Nominated for a Grammy award

2012: Release their fourth studio album, *Battle Born*

CHAPTER TWO

THE WHEELERS AND DEALERS

Behind every successful artist in the music industry is a manager who plays a vital role. He or she looks after all of the artist's money matters, steering their career. Band managers also act as the first point of contact for record labels, concert promoters and talent scouts.

Shaping careers

Often the first step on any band or singer's road to success is getting a manager. Sometimes, a friend or family member acts as an artist's manager in the early days. They work hard to build interest in the artist's music. Yet many bands find more success by employing an experienced manager with more knowledge of the music industry. They can then steer their artist in the right direction, whether by landing vital gigs at popular venues or by booking time in a recording studio to make their first demo.

Managers spend a lot of their time on the phone, booking gigs, arranging tours and drumming up interest in their acts from record labels.

Contacts

There's an old saying: 'it's not what you know, but who you know'. Most experienced managers have a bulging contacts book full of phone numbers of music industry professionals. They use this to get in touch with talent scouts and record label executives, encouraging them to attend gigs with a view to signing their artists.

Pay and play

When deciding whether to represent a new artist, managers have to weigh up whether they think they can make money from the relationship. If a band is successful, the manager could also become very rich. If they flop, the manager will struggle to pay his own bills. This is because most managers earn 15 to 20 per cent of an artist's earnings from record sales, concerts and merchandise (such as selling T-shirts).

The go-to man

As an artist's career develops, the manager's role is almost never-ending. They handle everything so that the artist doesn't have to. Some managers also have creative input into a band's look, sound or artistic direction. They are there not just to deal with an artist's affairs, but also to guide their career.

Management

If a band is offered a recording contract, the role of the manager is to negotiate with the record label on their behalf. Once a deal is done, the manager then liaises with the record label. He or she handles any requests for access to the artist, such as proposed radio interviews or television appearances.

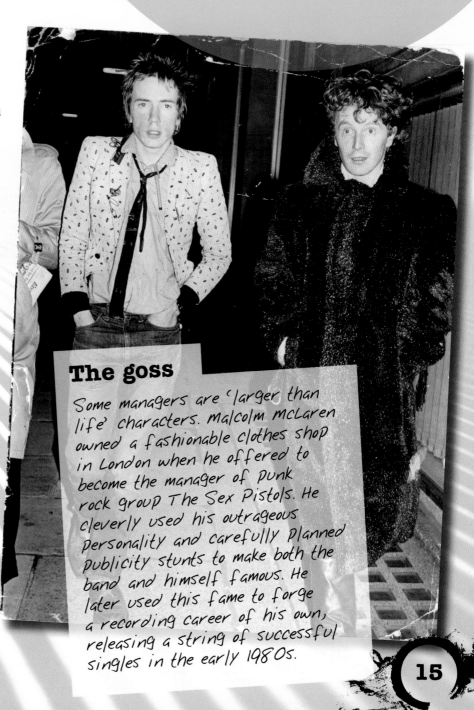

The goss

Some managers are 'larger than life' characters. Malcolm McLaren owned a fashionable clothes shop in London when he offered to become the manager of punk rock group The Sex Pistols. He cleverly used his outrageous personality and carefully planned publicity stunts to make both the band and himself famous. He later used this fame to forge a recording career of his own, releasing a string of successful singles in the early 1980s.

SIGNING UP

For any artist, signing a contract with a record label is a step towards fulfilling their dreams. It means that they will be releasing a single or album and could be on their way to stardom. But what do contracts include, how are they negotiated and what does the small print mean?

Signing your first recording contract is a life-changing moment for any musician. It means you could be on your way to superstardom!

Deal or no deal

A recording contract is a binding legal agreement between an artist and a record label. Once a contract is signed, the artist must produce a number of music releases for the label such as singles and an album. In return, the artist will be paid a certain amount of money depending on the success of a release.

Cash back

The artist may also be given a lump sum of money up front, called an 'advance'. In the past, many artists were paid large advances. Today, big advances are rare, and any money paid up front by the record label is usually then taken from future sales.

Profit share

Recording contracts have changed a lot in the last decade. Due to a fall in music sales, record labels usually offer short contracts to new artists. Contracts are often for just a year (in which the band or singer will make their first album), with an option to extend it if things go well.

Royalty rates have also changed. In the past, an artist might be paid 15 to 20 per cent of all revenues from record sales. Now, many labels offer a simple 50/50 split of all profits.

Setting the rules

No two recording contracts are ever the same. Deals can be exclusive. This means that they tie the artist to that record label alone for a set period of time. Other deals are flexible. They cover one 'territory' (a country or continent, such as Europe, or the whole world) and vary in length from 12 months to several years.

terms for themselves and limit any potential losses in case the artist's releases don't sell well. That's because only a small number of the artists and bands signed by record labels are ever successful enough to make serious amounts of money. As managers and labels rarely see eye-to-eye, contract negotiations can be long and drawn out.

Long negotiations

It is the responsibility of the artist's manager and advisors to try and get the best deal for their band. Record labels negotiate the best possible

The goss

Sometimes, the numbers involved in a recording contract for a big name artist can be staggering. In March 2010, the relatives of deceased singer Michael Jackson signed a deal with Sony music Entertainment worth a reported US$250 million (£158 million). The deal gave the major label the rights to the singer's entire back catalogue of music, plus three albums worth of unreleased songs. It was reported to be the biggest recording contract in the history of music.

Michael Jackson's music was so popular that his relatives signed a new contract with record label Sony after he died.

17

Breaking up

Record and management contracts are binding legal agreements. When band mates argue or someone leaves to go it alone, things can get very messy. That's certainly what happened to R&B supergroup Destiny's Child between 1999 and 2001.

Band beginnings

The members of Destiny's Child formed their first group as teenagers in Houston, Texas, in the early 1990s. Led by singer Beyoncé Knowles, the group also included rapper LaTavia Roberson and singers Kelly Rowland and LeToya Luckett. Beyoncé's father, Matthew Knowles, saw they had talent and offered to be their manager.

The only way is up

In 1997, Destiny's Child signed their first contract with Columbia Records. Within a year, they were regulars in the top ten of the Billboard charts and had recorded their debut album, *Destiny's Child*. The album's lead single, *No,No,No,* sold over one million copies in the USA alone.

Difficult times

Despite the band's worldwide success, LaTavia Roberson and LeToya Luckett weren't happy. They thought that the band's manager, Matthew Knowles, didn't have the group's best interests at heart. They wanted to hire a new manager. To do this, they would need to get out of their contract with Knowles.

Survivors

What followed was a very angry split. With Beyoncé and Kelly Rowland's blessing, Matthew Knowles recruited two new singers to replace Roberson and Luckett. The two original band members were furious and in March 2000, decided to sue Knowles, Beyoncé and Kelly Rowland for breach of contract. They used newspaper, radio and television interviews to put across their side of the story.

Destiny's Child in 2000, after LaTavia Roberson and LeToya Luckett left the band.

No, No, No!

Beyoncé and Kelly Rowland hit back. They accused their former band mates of being more interested in money than in Destiny's Child. A bitter 'war of words' developed. Yet despite the arguments, the band continued to be hugely successful – something that frustrated Roberson and Luckett even more.

Peacetime

In 2000, Roberson and Luckett agreed to drop their lawsuit for a payment of hundreds of thousands of dollars. Luckett and Roberson tried to kick-start their career by forming a new band, but it was unsuccessful. The new Destiny's Child secured a massive worldwide hit with the 2001 single *Survivor* and the album of the same name.

TIMELINE: Destiny's Child

1991: Beyoncé, Kelly Rowland and LaTavia Roberson form their first group, Girl's Tyme, as teenagers in Houston, Texas

1993: LeToya Luckett joins the group

1997: Change their name to Destiny's Child and sign to Columbia Records

1998: Release their debut album, *Destiny's Child*

1999: Roberson and Luckett removed from the group

2000: Roberson and Luckett drop their lawsuit against Beyoncé and Kelly Rowland

2001: Destiny's Child release their biggest selling album, *Survivor*

2004: Release their final album, *Destiny Fulfilled*

19

THE BIG PLAYERS

The music industry is dominated by a handful of powerful record labels. Known as 'major labels', these companies have enormous power to sign up the world's biggest stars and effectively control well over 90 per cent of global music sales.

A boom in record sales between 1950 and 2000 helped top record labels to become vast, multinational organisations with offices around the world.

Expansion

Initially, a handful of companies manufactured and distributed vinyl records. As buying records became popular in the 1950s and 1960s, these companies grew quickly. Many set up 'sub-labels' to handle different types of music and re-invested the huge sums earned from record sales into signing new bands and singers. This made the companies even bigger and made sure that smaller labels couldn't compete with them.

Contraction

Over time, many of the major labels have changed. Some have become larger by buying successful independent labels such as Motown, Island and A&M, while others have joined forces to make vast global corporations. At the end of the 1980s, there were six major labels – Warner Brothers, EMI, BMG, PolyGram, Sony and Universal.

The goss

Bizarre Inc were one of the most successful dance acts of the early '90s and were touted for great things when they signed to major label Mercury (a division of Universal) in 1996. Unfortunately, things didn't turn out well. The act made one album for Mercury, which sold poorly. To this day, the musicians behind the band, Andrew Meecham and Dean Meredith, are still in debt to the label. Until this debt is repaid, they will never make any money out of their Bizarre Inc music.

Major players

Today, there are just three major labels, Warner Music Group, Sony Music Entertainment and Universal Music Group. These large groups of companies own many different types of record labels all around the world. Many of these multinational corporations also have interests in other areas of the entertainment industry, such as television and film production. Sony is also one of the world's biggest manufacturers of electronic equipment.

Domination

Many artists dream of signing to a major label, because it is these huge corporations that have the money and big marketing teams to successfully promote their releases. You stand little chance of making it big unless you are contracted to one of these 'majors'.

Criticism

Some musicians are critical of major labels, saying that these companies are not interested in music unless it will sell in huge numbers. That's why some bands prefer to sign with smaller independent labels. These companies often share their passion for alternative sounds and do not require them to sell as many records.

U2 signed to independent label Island Records in 1980. Island is now part of Universal Music Group — one of only three major labels.

Warner Brothers versus Prince

Relationships between artists and record labels don't always run smoothly. The history of music is full of musicians falling out with their labels. So what happens when stars and labels go head to head?

At the height of his dispute with Warner Brothers, Prince was one of the highest-selling artists of the time.

Successful start

In the 1990s, American singer Prince and major label Warner Brothers were involved in one of the biggest battles the music industry had ever seen. The artist had been signed to the label since 1978, when they released his debut album *For You*. He quickly became one of the biggest soul and funk stars of the 1980s, releasing many successful albums that made him – and Warner Brothers – a lot of money.

Quantity versus quality

As the 1980s turned into the 1990s, Prince and Warner Brothers began to fall out. Prince wanted to release as much music as possible, while the label thought that more money could be made from fewer, higher quality releases. Prince believed that the label was deliberately limiting his artistic freedom. By 1993, the relationship between the singer and his record label was damaged beyond repair.

Protest symbol

As a protest, Prince refused to allow Warner Brothers to use his name on releases. He insisted that he was credited on his records, CDs and press releases as a symbol he'd designed himself (later called 'the love symbol'). Understandably, Warner Brothers weren't impressed and refused to release some of his music. The battle lines had been drawn.

Chaos and disorder

Prince was desperate to get out of his deal with Warner Brothers, but his contract stated that he still owed them four albums' worth of material. To run down his contract more quickly, Prince rapidly recorded the required number of albums and demanded that Warner Brothers release them.

Lasting legacy

Prince's battle with Warner Brothers has given other successful musicians the belief that they can take on record labels and win if they are unhappy with their deals. British singer George Michael fought a high profile court case with Sony Music in the late 1990s and early 2000s, while American country music star Tim McGraw sued Curb Records and Curb sued McGraw in 2011–2012. McGraw won — and left Curb.

Freedom

Warner Brothers agreed to Prince's request and released four new albums between 1994 and 1996. The label feared that the music would not sell well, and they were correct. Prince was very happy – he was now free.

New direction

Since getting out of his deal with Warner Brothers, Prince has released many of his albums himself and will only sign one-album deals with labels. His album, *20Ten*, was given away for free.

TIMELINE: Prince

1976: Records first demo tape in home city of Minneapolis

1978: Signs to Warner Brothers and releases his debut album, *For You*, aged 19

1993: Falls out with Warner Brothers and changes his name to a symbol

1996: Final Warner Brothers album, *Chaos and Disorder*, released

2014: More albums in the pipeline

SMALL IS BEAUTIFUL

Despite the dominance of the major labels, there is still enough room for smaller record labels to survive and thrive. These are the 'independents', the underground labels of the music industry.

Going underground

Independent record labels are the innovators of the music industry. They are usually founded by music fans or businessmen with a passion for alternative music and provide a voice for artists with less mainstream appeal. Independent labels often focus on one musical style or scene, for example dance music, indie-rock or folk.

Flexible friends

Because they are smaller, independent labels cannot offer artists huge contracts. They may just sign a particular record by an artist – for example, an album or single – rather than commit to a longer, more expensive deal. Yet independent labels offer artists something else: the complete freedom to express themselves creatively.

The goss

Millionaire businessman Sir Richard Branson (above) is now most famous for being the owner of Virgin Airlines, but he initially made his money through forming his own record label. Virgin Records was set up to release interesting rock music in the early 1970s, but quickly became a massive worldwide success. Although it regularly achieved both big sales and chart success, Virgin primarily released music by artists considered too alternative for the majors.

Independents' talent

The independents also serve another purpose: identifying exciting new talent. The people who run independent labels are usually good at spotting new musical trends. They pride themselves in offering opportunities to up-and-coming artists who may not attract the attention of major labels. Some of these artists may go on to sign for major labels later in their careers, but only after proving successful on an independent label.

Do it yourself

To set up your own independent record label you need passion, determination and some great music to release. Many independents have grown from such small origins to become massive success stories, taking underground music into the charts. XL Recordings were responsible for launching the careers of alternative dance acts such as The Prodigy and Basement Jaxx in the 1990s, before scoring worldwide success with singer-songwriter Adele.

Get creative

Many artists appreciate this creative support more than the money they would get from a major label because it allows them to make music from the heart. Others may be given a chance by an independent after being rejected by a major label. There are also artists whose music is considered too experimental for the mainstream, but who are able to make a living thanks to the support of independent labels.

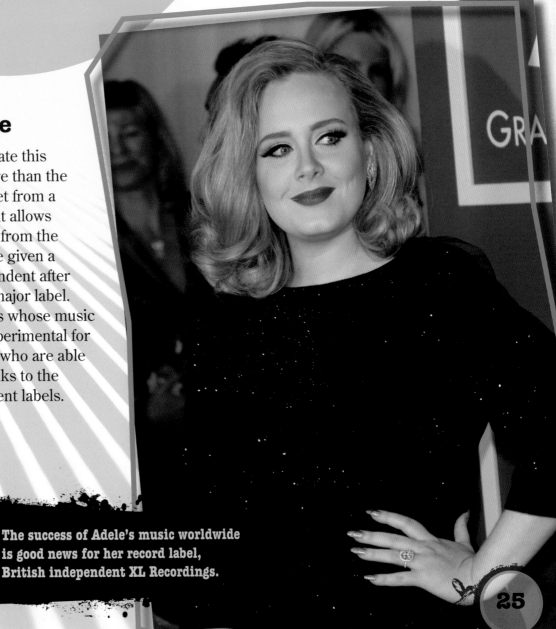

The success of Adele's music worldwide is good news for her record label, British independent XL Recordings.

CHAPTER THREE

THE RECORD MAKERS

Before artists can step into the studio and make records, they need some solid musical ideas that can be turned into strong tracks or songs. These ideas can come from a range of sources, from the discovery of a catchy tune while sitting at a piano to the break-up of a relationship.

Songwriting is harder than it looks, but a catchy song can be the difference between success and failure.

Songwriters

Ever since the earliest days of the music industry, many pop performers and major record labels have relied on the talents of professional songwriters. These are often talented musicians with a good ear for a tune, but perhaps less talent for performing. Because songwriters receive a 'royalty' every time one of their songs is recorded, sold or played on the radio, it can be a lucrative career.

Hit makers

Professional songwriters are still a huge part of the music industry today. Many pop stars – from Beyoncé and Leona Lewis to Justin Timberlake and Katy Perry – rely on music written by these specialists. Many top songwriters can earn almost as much as the stars they write songs for.

Like many pop singers, Leona Lewis performs songs that are written by professional songwriters.

Jam on it

There are hundreds of different ways to write songs, and each artist has their own preferred method. Some prefer to start with the music rather than a set of words. Others write songs by 'jamming' with their band members – playing around with sequences of chords and guitar riffs until an idea forms.

Divine inspiration

Many top performers write their own songs. These songs are often based on personal experiences, for example something that has happened in their life. Other performers, particularly rappers, write lyrics commenting on things happening in the world around them, such as global events or life in their neighbourhood.

The goss

Cathy Dennis had a successful pop career in the early 1990s, scoring chart success with a number of catchy songs. But it was when she stopped performing and turned her attention to songwriting full-time that her career really took off. Since 2000, she has written eight UK and US number one hits, including Britney Spears' Toxic, Kylie Minogue's Can't Get You Out of My Head and Katy Perry's I Kissed a Girl.

Technology

In the worlds of hip-hop and dance music, many musicians use high-tech electronic equipment to help them write songs. They begin by building a catchy groove or rhythm using a sampler and drum machine, then build a track around that. This method of working is particularly popular with rappers, who generally write lyrics to fit an instrumental track created for them by a music producer.

Rappers such as OutKast's Big Boi often get inspiration for song lyrics from the world around them.

American Idiot

Inspiration for music can come from all sorts of different places. In the 1960s and 1970s, many bands picked a theme and devised lavish 'rock operas' around them. Known as a concept album, this idea had all but died out when American punk-rockers Green Day got together in 2003 to record what would become their most famous work: *American Idiot*.

Green Day reinvented the 'rock opera' concept album with *American Idiot*, their most successful album to date.

Setback

Green Day were already a hugely successful band when they headed into the studio in 2003 to record a new album. The album was to be the long-awaited follow-up to 2000's big-selling *Warning*. By the middle of the year, they'd recorded enough tracks for a new album entitled *Cigarettes and Valentines*, but disaster struck when the master tapes were stolen. Instead of re-recording the tracks, they decided to try and come up with a new album from scratch over the next three months.

Breakthroughs

It was a great decision. Initially they struggled, managing just one complete song in the first two weeks of recording. Soon a breakthrough came when lead guitarist Billie Joe Armstrong heard bassist Mike Dirnt recording a 30-second song all on his own. Armstrong decided to do the same, and drummer Tre Cool quickly followed suit. They started to join all these 30-second tracks together and soon had a string of short songs called *Homecoming*.

Punk rock opera

This new approach to songwriting inspired Armstrong, who suggested the idea of making their new album a contemporary punk take on the rock opera concept. Armstrong sold it to the band as their own version of a 'musical' play, where the story is told through words and music. The band liked the idea, and got to work on another set of tracks.

Story time

As the songwriting sessions continued, Armstrong began to develop a story for the album. The songs focused on the life of a central character called Jesus of Suburbia, who was the American Idiot referred to in the album's title. He left his small American

New methods

American Idiot was the first time that Green Day had tried to write a concept album, and it excited them. Armstrong insisted that they were ambitious and tried new songwriting methods. When it came to recording, they spent a lot of time layering up different types of guitars to get a loud sound. The results were remarkable.

hometown, moved to a big city and faced a personal battle between love and rage. The story gave the band a solid creative framework and they set about finishing the songs as quickly as possible.

American heroes

American Idiot was a huge success when it was released in 2004 and has since been hailed as Green Day's best-ever album. It has so far sold more than 14 million copies worldwide, including six million CDs in the USA. In 2010, it was turned into a stage musical and performed on Broadway in New York City.

TIMELINE: Green Day

1987: Green Day forms in East Bay, California, USA
1990: Release their debut album *39/Smooth*
1994: Sign to label Reprise Records
2000: Album *Warning* sells 500,000 copies worldwide

2003: Recording on *American Idiot* begins
2004: *American Idiot* reaches number one in the American and British album charts
2012 Three studio albums released. They continue to write new songs

THE RECORDING STUDIO

The recording studio is at the heart of music production. It's where song ideas are turned into fully-fledged tracks, ready to be sold to the public. It's a complex process that involves a number of trained technicians, whose job it is to make the music sound as great as possible.

Making an album in a recording studio can be a long and drawn-out process.

Music producers have an important role – it's their job to make sure band recordings sound the best they can.

Space is the place

Recording studios can vary in size and shape. Some studios, such as Abbey Road in London or The Powerhouse in New York City, are world famous for the quality of their facilities. Others, such as the Moles Studio in Bath, UK, are famous for being small and comfortable. All studios are split into a number of rooms. There is usually a live room (sometimes referred to as the studio) and a control room.

Going live

The live room is set up to record live performances. With the help of a studio engineer or sound technician, bands or artists set up their instruments and microphones at the start of a recording session. They may then run through a few songs to make sure that everything is working and the sound is as they like it. If they're happy, the day's recording session can begin.

The producers

The most important person in the control room is the producer, who is assisted by a number of sound engineers. It's the producer's job to help the artist make the best record possible.

The goss

Marilyn Manson (below) got more than he bargained for when he asked Nine Inch Nails frontman Trent Reznor to produce his 1996 album Antichrist Superstar. At one point, the producer was so frustrated by how badly the recording sessions were going that he smashed up one of Manson's guitars!

In control

The control room is the heart of the studio. All music played in the live room is recorded in the control room, which is set up to shape and polish the sound to get the best possible finished 'mix'. A typical control room includes a mixing desk for recording sound, a computer workstation and a number of other pieces of high-tech music equipment.

The long haul

Recording a great song or album can be a long process. It can take even the best bands and singers a number of attempts, or 'takes', to get the best recording. On top of this, many bands also record 'overdubs'. These are extra instruments, backing vocals or special effects that help to give the finished track depth. Because of this, it can take several days to record a song and weeks or months to make an album.

Sound wizards

Good producers are experienced musicians with a wide technical knowledge of how recording equipment works. They carry out the artist's instructions, but also suggest solutions to problems or things to try that might help to improve the song. Top producers can earn huge fees for their services.

31

Sunset Sound Recorders

If you're a big star or world-famous band, you can take your pick of the world's recording studios. That means looking for the studio that has the best equipment and a reputation for delivering brilliant sound recordings. Few studios have quite as good a track record as Hollywood's Sunset Sound.

Pet Sounds

The first classic pop album recorded at Sunset Sound was The Beach Boys' 1966 album Pet Sounds. The album's producer, Beach Boys member Brian Wilson, used the studio's cutting-edge recording facilities to create tracks with many layers of sparkling sounds. It was called a landmark recording and made Sunset Sound Recorders the most in-demand recording studio in the world. It is still in demand today.

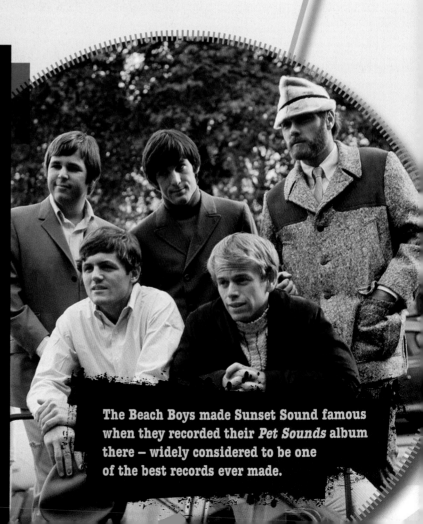

The Beach Boys made Sunset Sound famous when they recorded their *Pet Sounds* album there – widely considered to be one of the best records ever made.

Putting the magic into music

Sunset Sound was created in 1958, when Walt Disney Pictures' chief recording engineer Tutti Camarata suggested to his boss that he buy a recording studio. Walt Disney wasn't interested, but Camarata decided to do it anyway. He bought an old car repair garage on Sunset Boulevard in Hollywood and set about converting it into a state-of-the-art studio. By 1962, it was complete and opened for business under the name Sunset Sound Recorders.

Super studio

In the early days, Camarata's studio picked up a lot of work from Disney. The film company decided to record a number of soundtracks there, including *Mary Poppins*, *Bambi* and *Bedknobs and Broomsticks*. At the time, its facilities were far superior to many of its leading competitors, including AIR Studios and Abbey Road (both in London). Because of this, pop and rock bands quickly scrambled to book time in Sunset's three studios.

Three sounds

Sunset Sound has three separate recording studios, each with its own characteristics

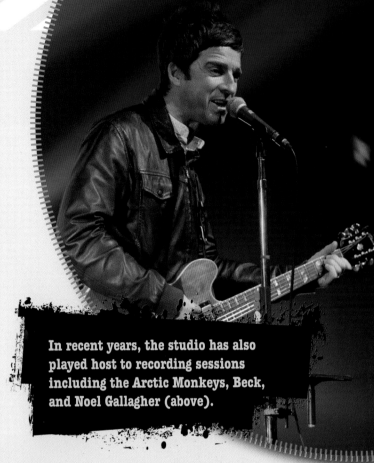

In recent years, the studio has also played host to recording sessions including the Arctic Monkeys, Beck, and Noel Gallagher (above).

and set-up. Studio One boasts a cutting-edge live echo chamber and over the years has been favoured by such artists as R&B star Macy Gray and The Rolling Stones. Studio Two is known for the quality of its live room. Studio Three, which has been favoured by Prince and recent punk-rockers Yellowcard, is smaller, cosier and capable of recording more moody sounds. To this day, many bands and artists are choosy about which of Sunset Sound's studios they record in.

TIMELINE: Sunset Sound

1958: Tutti Camarata leaves Walt Disney Pictures and looks for a space to set up his recording studio

1962: Sunset Sound Recorders opens in a converted garage off Sunset Boulevard in Hollywood

1965: The Beach Boys record their legendary album *Pet Sounds* at Sunset Sound

1972: Recording of The Rolling Stones'

Exile on Main Street

1982: Partner studio Sound Factory opens in Los Angeles

1995: Studio Two hosts sessions for Beck's *Odelay* album

2009: Arctic Monkeys record tracks for their *Humbug* album

2011: Former Oasis guitarist Noel Gallagher records his *High Flying Birds* album at Sunset Sound

SPREADING THE WORD

Once an album is recorded, the hard work really begins. That's because publicity and radio airplay can make or break a record. A good publicity and marketing campaign can be the difference between an artist making money and losing their recording contract.

Marketing masterclass

When a record is ready for release, a record label's marketing department takes over. They're responsible for raising interest in an artist or record so that their records sell well. There are many methods for doing this, from landing appearances on popular television shows to expensive advertising campaigns. They also include offering free track downloads and hosting 'playback' parties where fans can hear the album ahead of its release.

Playing the game

Not all artists enjoy talking to journalists. Because journalists can make or break a musician's career depending on what they write about them, many bands are naturally suspicious. Over the years, many

Bands such as Good Charlotte use media interviews to promote their concerts and albums.

Press corps

Most record labels employ press officers to seek positive coverage from newspapers, magazines, websites and radio stations. This could be in the form of interviews with the band, news articles or reviews of a record. A good review can make a huge difference to how many people buy a record, so press officers work hard to get copies of the album into the hands of the right journalists and bloggers.

rock stars have walked out of interviews or publicly criticised journalists. It is a difficult relationship because artists need publicity, while journalists need interviews to increase sales of their publication or attract more visitors to their website.

Plugging it

Radio plays a huge part in helping record labels to publicise their new releases. Securing regular airplay on radio stations is the job of radio 'pluggers'. They work hard to persuade radio stations to add tracks from their artists to 'playlists'. These playlists are important because tracks included on them are played more frequently.

The tastemakers

Club and radio DJs are important to the success of a record because they are regarded as tastemakers. If a popular DJ gets behind a record, it will be heard by many more people and could sell more copies. Because of this, DJs are regularly sent copies of records before anyone else.

Keyboard warriors

In the twenty-first century, Internet publicity has become a major part of marketing a record. Labels regularly send new releases to influential bloggers and post tracks on SoundCloud and YouTube. Online chat from potential buyers on websites such as Facebook and Twitter can also help to boost sales. Nowadays, positive online coverage is more important than the support of music magazines and newspapers.

The goss

In 2011, R&B star Rihanna (above) was heavily criticised by journalists for the way she dressed. They said that she wore clothes that were too revealing and that she was a bad role model for young fans. She used an interview to hit out at her critics, stating that she was just 'being herself'. She also said that fans should not copy her.

GLOBAL GROOVE

The music industry has always been a huge international industry, but rarely has that been as true as it is now. Artists and record labels focus on promoting their records all around the world through marketing trips and live tours.

Made in the USA

The biggest number of CDs and music downloads are sold in the USA. Traditionally, Americans preferred to buy actual CDs but, like the rest of the world, they now buy most of their music through digital download services. No artist will ever truly be a global star until they've 'made it' in the USA. Robbie Williams is a massive star in the UK, Europe and Australia, but he's never sold that many records in the USA – something he has fought to change for the last decade.

Asian power

Outside of the USA, the world's other music superpower is Japan. Despite a sharp slump in the sale of CDs in Japan in 2014, Japanese people love music and frequently spend more per person on CDs, downloads and concert tickets than those in the USA or Europe.

Big in Japan

Because of the strength of the Japanese music scene, record labels see it as a key market. Bands frequently head over to the country on promotional tours, playing venues such as Tokyo's massive Budokan Arena and festivals such as Fuji Rock. Japan is also a top destination for many DJs. The country's club scene is very strong and popular DJs can earn big money playing over there.

On the road

Concert or DJ tours are of vital importance to artists, whether they're huge stars or new artists. This is not just because playing concerts or performing DJ sets in a country is a good way to sell records. These days, fewer albums and singles are sold than in previous years. Because of this, artists rely on revenue from ticket sales and appearance fees to earn a living.

The goss

Between 1991 and 1993, American rocker band Guns 'N' Roses travelled the world in one of the longest concert tours in history. Over the course of two years, they played an amazing 193 shows in 27 different countries. That's roughly one concert every four days!

Japanese people love music and the country is home to some of the biggest music festivals in the world.

Mega bucks

The biggest bands and singers in the world can make huge amounts of money from world tours. Lady Gaga's *Monster Ball* tour, which took place between 2009 and 2011, raised more than US$227 million from ticket sales, while U2 earned over US$736 million from their 2009–2011 world tour.

Globe trotting

With such big numbers involved, it's no wonder that big rock and pop stars are keen to tour the world. These tours can be long and tiring, taking in dates on five continents over six months or a year. In the past, bands found time to record a new record in between tours. Now, they release a new album and then spend at least a year promoting it.

Guns 'N' Roses guitarist Slash once played 193 concerts in two years!

TELEVISION STARS

Ever since the 1960s, television has played a role in making and breaking music stars. Now, thanks to 24-hour music stations and reality TV shows, the boundaries between television and music are blurred.

Pick of the pops

In the 1960s, The Beatles made a huge splash in the USA after their appearance on a popular chat show. British broadcaster the BBC launched its own weekly show called *Top of the Pops* to cash-in on the popularity of pop music. Until it ended in the 2000s, *Top of the Pops* was one of the most watched television music shows in the world.

All change

The relationship between music and television changed profoundly in the 1980s with the launch of cable and satellite channels entirely devoted to music videos. Channels such as MTV and VH1 became hugely popular with teenagers, prompting record labels to spend more and more money on making videos.

Big budgets

Nowadays, music videos are integral to the success of any major music artist. A popular music video is watched many millions of times, not just on television but also on popular websites such as YouTube. As a result, record labels now spend vast sums on making videos and hiring expensive directors. They spend huge amounts of money on costumes, hair and make-up to ensure that everything looks perfect.

Many big stars spend more on making music videos than it costs to make a movie.

The goss

The Guinness World Record for the most expensive music video of all time is held by Michael and Janet Jackson. The clip for their 1995 single 'Scream' cost over US$7 million. The most costly video of recent times is Britney Spears' 'Work B——' which cost $6.5 million.

The world's got talent

The launch of the British television talent contest *Popstars* in 2001 started a new trend in music: television shows turning ordinary people into music stars. The series was the idea of former Spice Girls manager Simon Fuller and experienced record label executive Simon Cowell. They wanted to give television viewers a chance to watch a new pop group being created. They hoped that viewers would go out and buy their releases at the end of the series. They were proved correct – and it was the beginning of a new global trend.

A dream come true

Reality TV shows such as *Popstars*, *Pop Idol*, *American Idol* and *The X Factor* offer ordinary talented people a chance to fulfil their dreams of stardom. In turn, these would-be stars offer record labels an easy way of making money. The shows' popularity almost guarantees the winner a number one hit record, providing the record labels with huge sales and the potential to create a money-spinning global superstar.

Thanks to hit TV shows such as *American Idol* and *The X Factor*, Simon Cowell has changed the music industry forever.

Reality stars

Reality TV shows have made a lot of money for record labels and launched the careers of a number of genuine stars. One Direction and Leona Lewis are now household names on both sides of the Atlantic thanks to their success on *Britain's Got Talent* and the *The X Factor*.

MTV

The launch of music television station MTV in 1981 had a profound effect on the music industry. Within a decade, television had replaced radio as the number one promotional tool for music.

Music television

On 1 August 1981, a brand new cable television station spluttered into life in New Jersey, USA. With the famous words 'ladies and gentlemen, rock and roll', MTV was born. Following cleverly changed footage of the Moon landings (with the US flag replaced by a brightly-coloured MTV logo), the first music video on the station flickered onto the screen: *Video Killed the Radio Star* by Buggles.

Sales boom

MTV's impact was almost instant. Within weeks of the station going on air, local record shops were swamped with requests for tracks that had been played on the station. Record sales began to rise as rapidly as MTV's viewing figures.

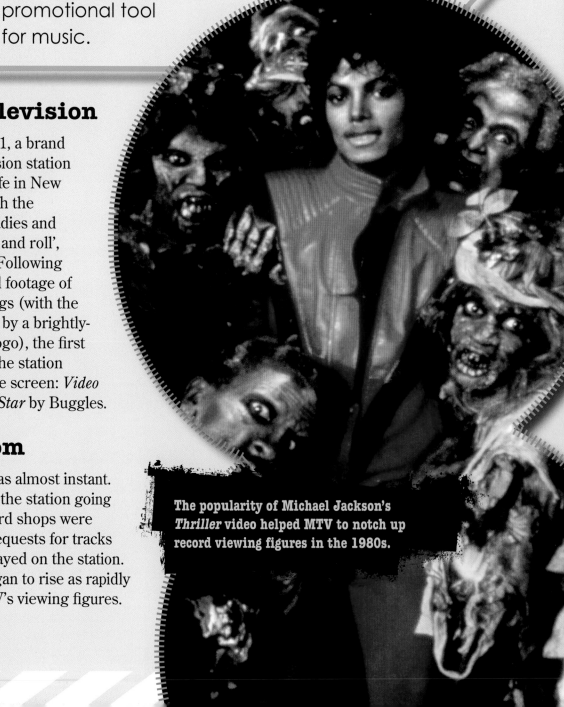

The popularity of Michael Jackson's *Thriller* video helped MTV to notch up record viewing figures in the 1980s.

Music with pictures

MTV was the idea of television executives Robert Pittman and John Lack. Having previously experimented with half-hour or hour-long music shows, they believed that their 'radio with pictures' concept for a TV channel that played nothing but music videos would catch on with American teenagers. Their hunch was right.

Overnight success

It wasn't long before MTV was rolled out across the entire USA. Its impact was huge, as kids and teenagers rushed to watch its never-ending diet of rock and pop videos. In the early days, the station received a lot of criticism for not including enough videos by black artists. By 1983, it had changed its outlook to include tracks from black pop stars such as Michael Jackson.

Changing times

The success of MTV encouraged record labels to invest more time and money into making videos. Prior to the station's launch, videos were cheaply made and only a small number of artists bothered making them. When MTV took off, record labels began to spend more of their promotional budgets on videos, realising they could boost record sales.

Rapid expansion

MTV's launch quickly led to the creation of many other 24-hour television channels. VH1 began in 1985 to cater for an older audience, while MTV Europe launched on satellite television in 1987. Then, in 1992, MTV hit Japan – much to the delight of record labels keen to tap into the lucrative Japanese market.

Global appeal

Thanks to the early work of MTV, music television is now a global phenomenon. There are currently hundreds of dedicated music television stations worldwide. Each caters for different musical tastes – from alternative rock, to dance music and mainstream pop. Music videos are now as important to the industry as records and concerts.

TIMELINE: MTV

1981: MTV launches on a small cable service in New Jersey

1984: Dire Straits use the 'I want my MTV' slogan in their song *Money for Nothing*

1985: Sister channel VH1 launches

1987: MTV Europe launches with a live concert by Sir Elton John

1992: MTV Japan starts broadcasting MTV20, a 12-hour non-stop music video marathon

2009: Ditches most music videos in favour of music-themed reality TV shows, something that proves popular with viewers

2013: About 85% of American households with televisions receive MTV

THE CHANGING FACE OF MUSIC

The rise of the Internet and downloadable music has changed the music industry enormously over the last decade. But how are record labels and artists responding to this?

In addition to the radio, we can now listen to music on mobile telephones, computers and MP3 players.

Music everywhere

In the twenty-first century, access to music has never been greater. We can find it on television, over the Internet and on our smartphones. Music is everywhere, yet sales of records are falling and some artists are finding it harder than ever to make a living.

Napster time

The issues caused by the rise of MP3 music downloads have made business difficult for record labels and artists ever since the early 2000s. It was then that a service called Napster became famous for allowing people to swap music over the Internet illegally. While paid-for MP3 downloads from websites such as the iTunes Store and Amazon now vastly outnumber sales of CDs and vinyl records, record labels are making less money than ever from music sales.

Massive losses

The reason for the fall in music sales is simple: illegal file sharing. This means listeners ignoring music copyright by giving music away for free on the Internet. Music industry figures show that music sales are dropping by an average of six per cent every year, as more people search for free music. For the music industry, it's a worrying sign.

Streaming success

Over the last few years, the music industry has been looking for new ways of making money to replace revenues lost from record sales. It has cashed in on the popularity of Internet music and video services such as Spotify, Last.fm and YouTube, which allow people to listen to or watch tracks but not download them. Now, record labels and artists receive payments from these services to make up for lost sales.

Promo power

The Internet music boom has not been all bad news for labels and artists. The rise in music blogs and streaming services such as SoundCloud and Mixcloud has given them many new opportunities to promote their music. Now, if a song proves popular on social network sites such as Twitter and Facebook, it can quickly lead to a rapid increase in download sales.

SOUNDCLOUD

What's the score?

Artists are also discovering that there are a number of other ways to make money in the music industry. One is to let film or game makers use their songs. This is known as 'licensing'. It can be a huge money-spinner for artists, because they are paid a fee up-front and also a small amount per DVD or game sold. Some underground artists have managed to make a comfortable living thanks to this kind of use of their music.

The goss

In February 2014 iTunes sold its 25th billionth song download. The most downloaded song of all time is The Black Eyed Peas' 'I Gotta Feeling', released in 2009. By 2014 it had sold a staggering 15 million copies. Close behind it was 'Blurred Lines' by Robin Thicke.

GLOSSARY

alternative music music that is different to, and sometimes not as popular as, pop music

artistic freedom the ability of a musician to express him or herself in any way through their music

aspiring ambitious

backing vocals singing that can be heard in the 'background' of songs, usually used to support the lead vocal

breach of contract what happens when someone refuses to honour their contract, for example by refusing to do something

campaign an organised series of events with one central aim, for example raising awareness of the release of a new CD

contemporary punk punk music made at the present time

credited to be given 'credit' for something you've done, for example writing or producing a song

debut album the first album recorded and released by a band or musician

distribution the process of getting a product into stores or onto online services such as iTunes (known as 'digital distribution')

echo chamber a room specially designed to produce a repeating echo sound, used by musicians to get certain special effects

experimental music that pushes the boundaries, for example by using non-traditional instruments

global corporation a large business that owns many companies around the world

imprints a music industry term for record labels

independent label a record label that is not owned by one of the three major labels, often specialising in alternative or underground music

innovators people who do things differently, often before anyone else

lawsuit the documents prepared by lawyers when you attempt to sue someone

losses a financial term used to describe what happens when you don't sell enough of something to pay for the cost of making it

lyrics the words of a song

mainstream appeal music that appeals to a lot of people, for example big chart hits

marketing the process of raising awareness of a product, for example an artist, a band or an album

master tapes the first 'hard copy' of a finished song or album

multinational companies that have offices in many different countries around the world

negotiate discussion between two or more people with differing views. The idea of 'negotiations' is to reach a compromise that satisfies everyone involved

phonograph the first machine to record and play back sound, developed by American inventor Thomas Edison

press releases information sheets sent to music writers and CD reviewers

profits the money that's left from sales after all costs – for example making CDs, paying for distribution, and so on – have been covered. If something sells poorly, it's unlikely there will be any profit

promoters people who 'promote' a product or service for a living, for example music concerts or nightclub events

record label a company that specialises in producing, making and releasing music

record label executives the people who run major record labels – for example the chief executive and various heads of departments (marketing, distribution etc)

revenues money

reviews short articles about a new music release or concert, often including both praise and criticism

rock opera a rock music album where all the tracks are connected by one central theme or concept

royalties throughout the world, a 'royalty' is paid to any writer and performer when their song is played on the radio, shown on television or bought by a member of the public

sampler a digital device that allows musicians to lift – or 'sample' – short sections from previously recorded songs (for example some drums, or a guitar chord)

showcase set a short performance by a band containing their strongest or most popular songs

soul and funk two styles of American dance music that were popular between the 1960s and 1980s

sound technicians people who specialise in making sure that a live performance or music recording sounds as good as it can be

streaming services websites that allow users to play, or 'stream', songs or videos

studio engineer someone who works in a recording studio and knows a lot about how all the equipment works

sub-label a smaller record label that is owned by a larger record label, usually used to release alternative music in a particular style

sue to take someone to court in an attempt to win compensation. This is usually done if you believe they have broken the law or broken a contract

FURTHER READING

Books

Anna Britten: *Working in the Music Industry – How to Find an Exciting and Varied Career in the World of Music* (How To Books, 2009)

Randy Chertkow: *The DIY Music Manual – How to Record, Promote and Distribute Your Music without a Record Deal* (Ebury Press, 2009)

Donald S Passman: *All You Need to Know About the Music Industry* (Penguin, 2011)

Paul Rutter: *The Music Industry Handbook* (Routledge, 2011)

Websites

Find out more about the latest music, read gossip and get advice about how to make your own music at:
www.teenmusic.com

INDEX